Historical Research

in Music Therapy

A Bibliography

by

George N. Heller
The University of Kansas

and

Alan L. Solomon
University of Evansville

THE UNIVERSITY OF KANSAS
Department of Art and Music Education and Music Therapy
311 Bailey Hall
Lawrence, KS 66045-2344

1992

ii

TABLE OF CONTENTS

I. BOOKS

Atlee, Edwin A. *An Inaugural Essay on the Influence of Music in the Cure of Diseases*. Philadelphia: B. Greaves, Printer, 1804.

Benedict, Milo E. *What Music Does to Us*. Boston: Small and Maynard, 1924.

Brocklesby, Richard. *Reflections on Ancient Musick with Application to the Cure of Diseases*. London: M. Cooper, 1749.

Browne, Richard. *Medicina Musica*. 2nd ed. Nottingham, England: John Cooke, Printer, 1729. First edition, London: J. Pemberton, 1727.

Chamberlain, H. E. *Music and Mental Hygeine*. Sacramento, CA: State Department of Social Welfare, 1942.

Chomet, D. Hector. *The Influence of Music on Health and Life*. Translated by Laura A. Flint. New York: G. P. Putnam and Sons, 1875.

Diserens, Charles M. *The Influence of Music on Behavior*. Princeton, NJ: Princeton University Press, 1926.

Edwards, Eleanor M. *Music Education for the Deaf*. South Waterford, ME: The Merriam-Eddy Company, 1974.

Feldon, Thomas. *Music and Character*. London: Nicholson and Watson, Ltd., 1932.

Heline, Corinne Dunklee. *Healing and Regeneration Through Music*. Santa Barbara, CA: J. F. Rowny Press, 1943.

Licht, Sidney H. *Music in Medicine*. Boston: New England Conservatory of Music, 1946.

Mathews, Ruth Vendley. *You Need Music: The Power of Music to Make You Healthy, Happy, and Wise*. Chicago: Neil A. Kjos Co., 1941.

Mathews, Samuel. *On the Effects of Music in Curing and Palliating Diseases*. Philadelphia: P. K. Wagner, 1806.

Music Answers the Call. New York: National Foundation for Music Therapy, 1942-43.

Podolsky, Edward. *The Doctor Prescribes Music*. New York: Frederick A. Stokes, 1939.

_____. *Music for Your Health*. New York: Bernard Ackerman, 1945.

Raymond, Thomas. *Singing for Health*. London: C. W. Daniel, Ltd., 1922.

Rothery, Guy Cadogan. *The Power of Music and the Healing Art*. London: Paul, Trench, Trubner, and Co., 1918.

Savill, Agnes. *Music, Health, and Character*. New York: Frederick A. Stokes, 1924.

Schoen, Max. *The Effects of Music*. New York: Harcourt, Brace Co., 1927.

Schullian, Dorothy, and Max Schoen, eds. *Music and Medicine*. New York: Henry Schuman, Inc., 1948.

Seashore, Carl E. *The Psychology of Musical Talent*. Boston: Silver Burdett and Company, 1919.

Seymour, Harriet Ayer. *How to Use Music for Health*. Larchmont, NY: H. A. Seymour, 1939.

_____. *What Music Can Do for You*. New York: Harper & Brothers, 1920.

Seymour, Harriet Ayer, and E. E. Garrett. *In the Use and Practice of Musical Therapy*. New York: National Foundation of Musical Therapy, 1944.

Sigerist, Henry E. *Civilization and Disease*. Ithaca, NY: Cornell University Press, 1943.

Singer, Kurt. *Diseases of the Musical Profession*. New York: Greenberg, 1932.

Soibelman, Doris. *Therapeutic and Industrial Uses of Music*. New York: H. Wells, 1936.

Stoddard, Wilbur, and Helen Wells. *Music as a Healing Art*. New York: H. Wells, 1936.

Trotter, Thomas Henry Yorke. *Music and Mind*. New York: H. Doran Co., 1923.

The Use of Music in Hospitals for Mental and Nervous Diseases. New York: National Music Council, 1944.

Van de Wall, Willem. *Music in Correctional Institutions*. Albany, NY: J. B. Lyon Co., 1923.

_____. *Music in Hospitals*. New York: Russell Sage Foundation, 1936.

_____. *Music in Institutions*. New York: Russell Sage Foundation, 1936.

_____. *Music's Mission in Correctional Personality Reconstruction*. Albany, NY: J. B. Lyon, 1924.

_____. *The Music of the People*. New York: American Association for Adult Education, 1939.

_____. *The Utilization of Music in Prisons and Mental Hospitals:: Its Application in the Treatment and Care of the Morally and Mentally Afflicted*. New York: National Bureau for the Advancement of Music, 1924.

4

Vescelius, Eva A. *Music and Health.* New York: Goodyear Book Shop, 1918.

Washco, Alec, Jr. *The Effects of Music Upon the Pulse Rate, Blood Pressure, and Mental Imagery.* Philadelphia: Temple University, 1933.

II. BOOK CHAPTERS, PERIODICALS, NEWSPAPERS, YEARBOOKS, AND PROCEEDINGS

Ainlay, George W. "The Place of Music in Military Hospitals." *Etude* 63 (August 1945): 433, 468, 480.

Altschuler, Ira M. "The Case of Horace F." *MTNA Proceedings* (1946): 368-381.

_____. "Four Years' Experience with Music as a Therapeutic Agent at Eloise Hospital." *American Journal of Psychiatry* 100 (May 1944): 792-794.

_____. "Music Aid in Management of Psychotic Patients." *Journal of Nervous and Mental Disease* 94 (August 1941): 179-183.

_____. "Music in the Treatment of Neurosis: Theoretical Considerations and Practical Experience." *MTNA Proceedings* (1944): 155-163.

_____. "Music Served Up as Mental Medicine." *Baltimore Sun*, 17 January 1944.

_____. "Music Therapy: Retrospective and Perspective." In *Music Therapy 1952*, 3-18.

_____. "The Organism-As-A-Whole and Music Therapy." *Sociometry* 8 (August-November 1945).

_____. "The Part of Music in Resocialization of Mental Patients." *Occupational Therapy and Rehabilitation* 20 (April 1941): 75-86.

_____. "Past, Present and Future of Music Therapy." *Educational Music Magazine* 24 (January-February 1946): 16-17, 53-54.

_____. "Rational Music-Therapy of the Mentally Ill." *MTNA Proceedings* (1939): 153-157.

6

_____. "Report of Sub-Committee on Music Therapy." *MTNA Proceedings* (1945): 186-188.

Altschuler, Ira M., and Bessey H. Shebesta. "Music—An Aid in the Management of the Psychotic Patient." *Journal of Nervous and Mental Diseases* 94 (August 1941): 179-183.

Antrim, Dorothy K. "Healing Children with Music: Occupational Therapy with Musical Instruments." *Etude* 61 (October 1943): 651.

_____. "Music and the Battle of Life." *Etude* 61 (November 1943): 724.

_____. "Music Therapy." *Musical Quarterly* 30 (October 1944): 409-420.

Armstrong, William G. "Singing for Health." *Etude* 63 (July 1945): 375, 406.

Assaglioli, R. "Music as a Cause of Disease and as a Healing Agent." *International Review of Educational Cinematography* 5 (September 1933): 583-595.

Ballantine, J. C. "Music and Medicine." *St. Mary's Hospital Gazette* 46 (1942): 25-26.

Beardsley, G. L. "The Medical Uses of Music." *New England Medical Monthly* 2 (1882-1883): 214-216.

Bell, F. D., and Isa Maud Ilsen. "The Psychological Effect of Music in Tuberculosis Patients." *Modern Hospital* 25 (September 1925): 227.

Bennett, Victor. "Music and Emotion." *Musical Quarterly* 28 (October 1942): 406-414.

Benton-Mednikoff, Patricia. "Musical Therapy Used for Post-Operative Corrective Work in Orthopedics." *Occupational Therapy and Rehabilitation* 22 (June 1943): 13-139.

Berthoud, S. Henri. "A Cure Effected by Music." *Dwight's Journal of Music* 19 (13 April 1861): 10.

"Black Tom." *Dwight's Journal of Music* 22 (22 November 1862): 275.

Blackman, J. G. "Music and Medicine." *Medical Magazine* 1 (1892-1893): 628-637.

Blackwell, Ethel, and Gordon A. Neil. "Music in Mental Hospitals." *Occupational Therapy and Rehabilitation* 25 (December 1946): 243-246.

"The Blind as Tuners." *Dwight's Journal of Music* 38 (5 January 1878): 156-157.

"Blind Musicians in London." *Dwight's Journal of Music* 34 (16 May 1874): 228.

"The Blind Negro Boy Pianist." *Dwight's Journal of Music* 16 (11 February 1860): 364.

"The Blind School at Liverpool." *The Euterpiad: Or, Musical Intelligencer* 1 (11 November 1820): 130-131.

"Blind Tom." *Dwight's Journal of Music* 22 (8 November 1862): 250-252.

"Blind Tom." *Dwight's Journal of Music* 22 (8 November 1862): 254.

"Blind Tom." *Dwight's Journal of Music* 22 (24 January 1863): 340-341.

"Blind Tom." *Dwight's Journal of Music* 26 (27 October 1866): 336.

"'Blind Tom' Again." *Dwight's Journal of Music* 22 (22 November 1862): 267-268.

"'Blind Tom' and Done With." *Dwight's Journal of Music* 22 (6 December 1862): 286.

"Blindness and Music." *Dwight's Journal of Music* 37 (1 September 1877): 83-84.

Blumer, George Alder. "Music in Its Relation to the Mind." *American Journal of Insanity* 5 (1891-1892): 350-364.

Boguslawski, Moissaye. "Music as a Cure for Mental Depression." *Etude* 50 (July 1932): 469.

Bowers, Mabela. "A Music Program in a Residential School for Higher Grade Mental Defectives." *American Journal of Mental Deficiency* 50 (April 1946): 520.

Boxberger, Ruth. "Historical Bases for the Use of Music in Therapy." *Music Therapy 1961*, 125-166.

_____. "A Historical Study of the National Association for Music Therapy Inc." *Music Therapy 1962*, 133-197.

Braswell, Charles. "Psychiatric Music Therapy: A Review of the Profession." *Music Therapy 1961*, 53-64.

Braxton, Alembert W. "Music and Poetry: Their Relation to the Medical Life." *Indiana Medical Journal* 24 (May 1906): 425-426.

_____. "Music as a Therapeutic Agent." *New York Medical News* (29 October 1904).

Brierre de Boismont, A. "A Concert of Music by Hospitalized Mental Patients." *Medical Union* 7 (1860): 337-344.

Britain, H. H. "The Power of Music." *Journal of Philosophy7, Psychology, and Scientific Methidf* 5 (1908): 48-63.

Brown, Holbert H. "The Power of Music." *Journal of Philosophy, Psychology and Scientific Methods* 5 (1908): 352-357.

Brown, Ray E., H. M. Livingston, and Joel Williard. "Silent Music Soothes the Surgical Patient." *Modern Hospital* 72 (April 1949): 51.

Burdick, W. P. "The Use of Music During Anesthesia and Analgesia." *The American Yearbook of Anesthesia and Analgesia* (1916): 164-167.

Burris-Meyer, Harold, and Richmond L. Cardinell."The Place of Music in Healing." *Journal of the Acoustical Society of America* 17 (January 1946): 232-235.

Butterfield, Myrtle Alice. "How Music Study Has Helped the Sickly." *The Musician* 19 (July 1924): 23.

Caldeira, Filho, J. C. "Therapy by Means of Music." *Illustrated Medicine* 10 (May-September 1944): 49-51.

Campbell, F. "Therapeutic Influence of Music." *Good Housekeeping* 50 (January 1910): 12.

Carpuso, Alexander. "Written Responses in a Musical Situation as a Function of the Stability of Emotional Behavior." *Journal of General Psychology* 23 (1940): 289-304.

Cartwright, Harriet Gordon. "The Healing Art of Music." *Etude* 63 (February 1945): 81, 110.

_____. "More Musical Therapeutics." *Etude* 63 (March 1945): 136.

"Case Mental Excitement Allayed by Music." *American Journal of Insanity* 3 (1846-47): 149-150.

Cawston, Norman. "Music and Medicine." *South African Medical Journal* 6 (February 1932): 119.

Chendwith, R. "Music as Therapy for Convalescent Children." *Occupational Therapy and Rehabilitation* 25 (December 1946): 241-242.

Cherry, H., and I. M. Pallidin, "Music as a Supplement in Nitrous Oxide-Oxygen Anesthesia." *Anesthesiology* 9 (July 1948): 391-399.

Clair, Alicia Ann, and George N. Heller. "Willem van de Wall (1887-1953): Organizer and Innovator in Music Education and Music Therapy." *Journal of Research in Music Education* 37 (Fall 1989): 165-178.

Clapp, Arthur A. "Throbs and Thrills of Music: Their Moral and Medicinal Virtues." *Dominant* 21 (1913): 18-23.

Clark, K. S. "Using Music as a Healing Force." *The Playground* 17 (5 August 1923): 256.

Clendening, Logan. "Music Is Employed in Healing." *The Wisconsin State Journal*, 14 October 1937.

Codellas, Pan S. "The Evolution of Melotherapy: Music in the Cure of Disease." *California and Western Medicine* 32 (June 1930): 411-412.

"A Collegiate and Musical Institute for the Blind." *Dwight's Journal of Music* 29 (15 January 1870): 172-173.

Colville, W. J. "Music as a Healing Power: Practical Applications" *Music and Health* 1 (1914): 11-16.

"Columbia University to Heal Wounded by Music." *Literary Digest* 60 (1 March 1919): 59-62.

"Concerts of the Blind." *Dwight's Journal of Music* 28 (6 June 1868): 254.

Connery, Julia M. "A Demonstration in Voice Training." *The Volta Review* 21 (February 1919): 108-109.

Corning, James L. "The Musical Memory and Its Derangement (Amusia)." *Medical Record* 81 (1912): 51-62.

_____. "The Use of Musical Vibrations Before and During Sleep: A Contribution to the Therapeutics of the Emotions." *Medical Record* 14 (January 1899): 79-86.

Crampton, Marion W. "Musical Magic." *Occupational Therapy and Rehabilitation* 25 (December 1946): 207-209.

Cranshaw, Edith A. "Music and Medicine." *Choir* 8 (September 1917): 200-203.

"Curing Disease by Color and Music." *Review of Reviews* 41 (January 1910): 13.

Darrow, Alice-Ann, Alicia Clair Gibbons, and George N. Heller. "Music Therapy in *Dwight's Journal of Music*, 1853-1880: A Reflection of the Times." *Music Education for the Handicapped Bulletin* 2 (Fall 1986): 20-38.

_____. "Music Therapy Past, Present, and Future." *American Music Teacher* 35 (September-October 1985): 18-19, 33.

Darrow, Alice-Ann, and George N. Heller. "Early Advocates of Music Education for the Hearing Impaired: William Wolcott Turner and David Ely Bartlett." *Journal of Research in Music Education* 33 (Winter 1985): 269-279.

Davis, Frank Albert. "Music as a Part of the Occupational Therapy Programs in a Mental Hospital." *United States Veterans Bureau Medical Bulletin* 5 (March 1929): 223-226.

Davis, William B. "Music Therapy in Nineteenth-Century America." *Journal of Music Therapy* 24 (Summer 1987): 76-87.

_____. "Music Therapy in Victorian England: Frederick Kill Harford and the Guild of St. Cecilia." *Music Therapy Perspectives* 7 (1989): 17-22.

Davison, James T. "Music in Medicine." *The Lancet* 2 (October 1899): 1159-1162.

"The Deaf and Dumb Fond of Music." *The Euterpiad: Or, Musical Intelligencer.* 1 (10 March 1821): 200.

12

DeHorvath, Felice. "The Greeks and Musical Therapeutics." *Etude* 63 (September 1945): 489, 524.

"Demonstrations by Jennie Henderson." *The Volta Review* 30 (October 1928): 609-612.

Denbo, Doris. "Music for Your Pains." *American Magazine* 130 (September 1940): 68.

Densmore, Frances. "Music in the Treatment of the Sick by American Indians." *Hygeia* 1 (April 1923): 29-30.

_____. "The Use of Music in the Treatment of the Sick by American Indians." *Musical Quarterly* 13 (October 1927): 555-565.

_____. "What the Indians Knew about Music Therapy." *Musical Courier* 5-6 (15 March 1948).

Deutsch, Albert. "Will Music Cure the Insane? 'Master X' Case Still Stirs Debate on Music Therapy." *Science Digest* 19 (June 1946): 1-2.

Diserens, Charles M. "Reactions to Musical Stimuli." *Psychological Bulletin* 20 (1923): 173.

Dixon. J. H. "Music and Medicine." *Medical Magazine* 9 (1900): 290-300.

Donais, Darlene. "Music Sets the Stage for Recovery from Mental Diseases." *Modern Hospital* 61 (1943): 68-69.

Douty, Nicolas. "Music as Therapeutic Agency." *Etude* 63 (May 1945): 287.

Downes, Olin. "The Value of Music Therapy." *New York Times*, 21 October 1945, sec. 2, p. D1.

Dubb, A. "Medical Philately, Medical Melody: The Story of Medicine and Music, Part 2." *Adler Museum Bulletin* 6 (1880): 3-8.

13

Duffett, Frances L. "Voice Building." *The Volta Review* 21 (October 1919): 639-640.

Duncan, L. "Music, Medicine, and the Arts." *Medical Journal of Australia* 1 (February 1937): 290-293.

Dunton, W. R., Jr. "Recreation and Music Therapy." *Occupational Therapy and Rehabilitation* 25 (December 1846): 247-252.

Dunton, W. R., and H. F. Carleton. "Music Cataloging." *Archives of Occupational Therapy* 3 (1924): 289-294.

Dyer, T. F. "Music and Medicine." *Gentleman's Magazine* 37 (1886): 375-385.

Dykema, Peter W. "Music as Recreation." *The Playground* 17 (January 1924): 533.

_____. "Some Social Aspects of Music in Therapy." *MTNA Proceedings* (1945): 55-63.

Eaglesfield, C. C. "Pathological and Therapeutic Value of Music." *Catholic World* 73 (April 1901): 44-53.

Eby, Julia. "The Value of Music in a Psychiatric Institution." *Occupational Therapy and Rehabilitation* 22 (February 1943): 31-35.

Edwards, Landon B. "Music as Mind Medicine." *Virginia Medical Monthly* 4 (1877-1878): 920-923.

Edwards, W. M. "Treatment of Disease by Music." *American Medicine* 9 (1905): 305.

"The Effects of Music on Mind an Body." *Journal of Mental Science* 67 (April 1921): 162.

Eisenberg, Jacob. "Home-Made Music as a Social Therapeutic Agency." *The Musician* 40 (September 1935): 6, 8.

Elson, Louis C. "Music and Health." *Etude* 15 (January 1897): 12.

14

Emory-Jones, H. "Music as Medicine." *Philharmonic* 11 (November 1902): 263-268.

"Employment for the Blind: Piano Tuners." *Dwight's Journal of Music* 36 (15 April 1876): 211.

Engel, Carl. "Music in Medicine." In *Musical Myths and Facts*. London: Novello, Ener, and Co., 1876.

Erdman, Adolf Frederick. "Music Aids Anesthetist." *Scientific American* 149 (August 1933): 84.

_____. "The Silent Gramophone in Local Anesthesia and Therapy." *Anesthesia and Analgesia* 13 (November-December 1934): 70-71.

"An Experiment in Mental Hygiene." *Long Island Medical Journal* 17 (May 1928): 49-50.

Eyer, Ronald F. "New Science of Music Therapy Develops." *Musical America* 63 (25 January 1943): 8.

"Famous London Physician on the Healing Power of Music." *Etude* 42 (March 1925): 160.

Finck, A. W. "Music and Poetry: Their Relation to the Medical Life." *Forum* 25 (1898): 300-310.

Fineberg, Rebecca B. "Music in Therapy." *Music Publishers Journal* 4 (March-April 1946): 52.

Flower, B. O. "Music as Medicine." *Arena* 30 (September 1903): 323-325.

Foster, E. M. "Treatment of Disease by Music." *American Medicine* (1905).

Foster, Eugenie, and E. A. Gambie. "The Effect of Music on Thoracic Breathing." *American Journal of Psychology* 17 (1906): 406-414.

Fowler, Margaret Winslow. "Music as Medicine." *Coronet* 19 (January 1946): 140-143.

Fuller, Millicent Bowen. "Rhythm." *American Annals of the Deaf* 62 (May 1917): 257-261.

Fultz, Arthur F. "Music as Modality of Occupational Therapy." *War Medicine* 5 (March 1944): 139-141.

Garbett, Arthur S. "Music for the Hard of Hearing." *Volta Review* 45 (October 1943): 571-575.

Gardner, B. Bellamy. "Therapeutic Qualities of Music." *Music and Letters* (July 1944): 181-185.

Gaston, E. Thayer. "Functional Music—Review of Pertinent Research." *Music Journal* 7 (March-April 1949): 25, 56.

_____. "Motor-Visual Imagery in Tonal Thinking." *Music Educators Journal* 26 (February 1940): 79-81.

_____. "Music Education for Health." *Music Educators Journal* 31 (February-March 1945): 24-25.

_____. "Music in Therapy—A Re-Evaluation of Its Importance in Light of Recent Developments." *Bulletin of the National Association of Schools of Music* 25 (June 1947): 13.

_____. "Music in Therapy: A Review of Some Recent Research Literature." *MTNA Proceedings* (1949), 118-125.

_____. "Music Therapy." *Kansas Music Review* 7 (May 1945): 5, 13.

_____. "Musical Therapy." *Music Educators Journal* 35 (November-December 1948): 58.

_____. "Needed Research in the Psychology of Music Bearing on (1) Normal Human Living, (2) Abnormal or Pathological Living." *MTNA Proceedings* (1948).

16

_____. "Psychological Foundations for Functional Music." *American Journal of Occupational Therapy* 2 (February 1948): 1-8.

_____. "Values of Functional Music for Music Education." *Education* 69 (March 1949): 396-398.

Gatewood, Esther L. "Is There Evidence for the Therapeutic Use of Music?" *The Trained Nurse and Hospital Review* 69 (July 1922): 13-16.

_____. "Music in the Hospital." *Literary Digest* 72 (February 1923): 68-70.

_____ "The Psychology of Music in Relation to Anesthesia." *American Journal of Surgical Anesthesia* 35 (April 1921): 47-50.

Geddes, Kathleen R. "Music for the Hard of Hearing." *The Volta Review* (February 1920): 73-74.

Gether, Alice E. "Music for the Sick." *Music* 7 (1894-1895): 254-257.

Gibbons, Alicia Clair, and George N. Heller. "Music Therapy in Handel's England: Browne's *Medicina Musica*." *College Music Symposium* 25 (1985): 59-72.

Gilliland, A. R., and H. T. Moore. "The Immediate anbd Long-Time Effects of Classical and Popular Phonograph Selections." *Journal of Applied Psychology* 8 (1924): 309-323.

Gilliland, Esther Goetz. "Apollo, God of Music and Healing." *The Wheel* (May 1945).

_____. "Are You Making the Most of Music?" *Occupational Therapy and Rehabilitation* 25 (December 1946): 238-240.

_____. "The Healing Power of Music." *Music Educators Journal* 31 (September-October 1944): 18-20.

_____. "Music Can Heal—Try It on Yourself." *Pan Pipes of Sigma Alpha Iota* (April 1945).

_____. "Music for the War Wounded." *Music Educators Journal* 31 (April 1945): 24-25, 51.

_____. "Music Gains Acclaim as Therapy Aid." *Victor News* [of the General Electric X-Ray Corporation] (December 1945).

_____. "Music in Rehabilitation." *Illinois Music Educator* (May 1945).

_____. "Music in the Treatment of the Sick." *Hygeia* 22 (December 1944): 897.

_____. "Music the Healer." *Pan Pipes of Sigma Alpha Iota* (December 1944).

_____. "Today's Hospital Needs Music: It Lightens Labor, Speeds Recovery." *Hospital Managementt* 64 (Sepetember 1947): 116-120.

_____. "Unlocked Doors." *Illinois Parent Teachers Association Magazine* (November 1946).

Gilman, L., and Frances Paperte. "Music as a Psychyotherapeutic Agent." *Journal of Clinical Psychopathology* 10 (1949): 286-303.

Goldberg, Albert. "The Therapeutic Values of Music." *The Musical Digest* 13 (April 1928): 20, 69-70.

Graeve, Hildegard E. "The Musical Program in an Institution." *Proceedings of the American Association on Mental Deficiency* (1939): 228-233.

Green, Ray. "The Music Program in Veterans Administration Hospitals." *Music Library Association Notes* 5 (December 1947): 36-41.

_____. "Music in the Veterans Hospital." *Music Educators Journal* 34 (November-December 1947): 22-24.

Grothe, Edna W. "Music in Medicine." *Occupational Therapy and Rehabilitation* 5 (October 1926): 353-358.

Gruet, Jean Paul. "Hearing a Concert with My Feet." *The Volta Review* 20 (December 1918): 790-791.

Gutheil, Emil. "Musical Day Dreams." *Psychoanalytical Review* 22 (August 1935).

Hackett, Henry. "The Influence of Music Upon Mind and Health." *Choir* 21 (September 1930): 193-194.

Hadden, J. Cuthbert. "Music as Medicine." *Music* 9 (1896): 359-368.

_____. "Music as a Medicine." *New Music Review* 18 (1920): 140-142.

Hampton, Peter J. "The Emotional Element in Music." *The Journal of General Psychology* 33 (1945): 237-250.

Hanson, Howard. "A Musician's Point of View Toward Emotional Expression." *American Journal of Psychiatry* 99 (November 1942): 317-325.

_____. "Objective Studies of Rhythm in Music." *American Journal of Psychiatry* 101 (November 1944): 364-369.

Harding, J. W. "Music Takes First Place in Reconstruction Work." *Modern Hospital* 12 (June 1919): 404-406.

Harford, F. K. "Music and Illness." *The Lancet* 2 (1891): 43.

Harmon, Francis L. "The Effects of Noise Upon Certain Psychological and Physiological Processes." *Archives of Psychology* 23 (February 1933): 81.

Harrington, Arthur H. "Music as a Therapeutic Aid in a Hospital for Mental Diseases." *Mental Hygiene* 23 (October 1939): 601-609.

_____. "The Story of the State Hospital Pipe Organ." *Abstracts in Occupational Therapy* 6 (April 1927): 170.

Hawley, Oscar Hatch. "The Power of Music." *The Musician* 17 (1906): 540.

"Health and Musicianship." *Etude* 13 (October 1895): 221.

Heller, George N. "Ideas, Initiatives, and Implementations: Music Therapy in America, 1787-1848." *Journal of Music Therapy* 24 (Spring 1987): 35-46.

Hemmeter, John C. "Theodore Billroth, Musical and Surgical Philosopher: A Biography and Review of His Work on Psycho-Physiological Aphorisms in Music." *Bulletin of the Johns Hopkins Hospital* 11 (December 1900): 297-317.

Herman, A. L. "Hygiene of Music." *Journal of the American Medical Association* 31 (1898): 939.

Hill, A. C. "From the Note-Book of an Inspector." *The Volta Review* 20 (June 1918): 315-316.

Hoffman, B. "The Efficacy of Music in Hospitals." *The Trained Nurse and Hospital Review* 95 (September 1935): 212-214.

Howe, Bertha S. "The Influence of Music." *Jacobs' Orchestra Monthly* 2 (1911): 68-70.

Hubbard, G. R. "Musical Playground for Crippled Children." *Playground* 22 (July 1928): 701.

Huebner, Ilse. "Musical Aspects of Hemmeter." *Medical Life* 34 (April 1927): 224-226.

Hughes, C. W. "Rhythm, Medicine, and Health: A Historical Survey." *MTNA Proceedings* (1946), 350-355.

Humphreys, E. J. "Medical and Surgical Convalescence in Relation to Art and Music." *Clinical Medicine and Surgery* 24 (November 1934): 518-520.

Hunt, E. Ernest. "Singing and the General Health." *Etude* 34 (September 1916): 666.

Hyde, Ida H. "Effects of Music Upon Electrocardiograms and Blood Pressure." *Journal of Experimental Psychology* 7 (1924): 213-224.

Hyde, Ida H., and William Scalapino. "Influence of Music upon Electrocardiograms and Blood Pressure." *American Journal of Physiology* 46 (April 1918): 35-38.

Ilsen, Isa Maud. "Healing Music." *The Trained Nurse and Hospital Review* 77 (December 1926): 605-608.

_____. "How Music Is Used in Hospitals." *The Musician* 31 (May 1926): 15, 30.

_____. "Music as a Medicine and a Tonic in Restoring Health." *Modern Hospital* 34 (February 1930): 81-84.

_____. "The Value of Music in Hospitals." *Clinical Medicine and Surgery* 34 (October 1927): 765-768.

"Ingenuity of a Blind Man." *The Euterpiad: Or, Musical Intelligencer* 1 (9 June 1821): 43.

Isaacson, Charles D. "Music and Medicine." *Medical Review of Reviews* 24 (October 1918): 602-606.

_____. "Music—How It Affects Your Health." *The Music Bulletin* 16 (November 1931): 8-11.

Isham, A. C. "The Use of Song Parodies as Recreational Therapy for Mental Patients." *Occupational Therapy and Rehabilitation* 24 (1945): 259-261.

Jackson, J. "Music at Johns Hopkins." *American Journal of Nursing* 41 (1941): 1373-1375.

Jacoby, P. J. "Music Is in Tune with the Art of Healing." *Modern Hospital* 67 (1946): 60-61.

Jameson, Armen, and Samuel H. Jameson. "Musical Therapy in Social Control." *Sociology and Sociological Research* 17 (July-August 1933): 534-544.

Jennings, O. "Music as a Therapeutic Agent." *Lancet* 2 (1880): 794.

Jenesbury, E. G. O. "Musicians, Music, and Medicine." *St. Bartholomew's Hospital Journal* 45 (1938): 227-231.

Johnson, Robert E. "E. Thayer Gaston: Leader in Scientific Thought on Music in Therapy and Education." *Journal of Research in Music Education* 29 (Winter 1981): 279-286.

Jordan, Sarah Allen. "Rhythm as an Aid to Voice Training." *The Association [Volta] Review* 2 (February 1900): 16-19.

Kalms, Martha A. "Differences in the Music Program of Private and State Hospitals" *Occupational Therapy and Rehabilitation* 21 (October 1942): 294-296.

_____. "Music for Mental Patients." *The Modern Hospital* 54 (1940): 72.

_____. "Music in Mental Hospitals." *Occupational Therapy and Rehabilitation* 10 (December 1931): 381-385; see also *Disques* 3 (September 1932): 295-297.

_____. "Musical Therapy." *Occupational Therapy and Rehabilitation* 19 (June 1940): 181-186.

Kane, Evan O'Neill. "Phonograph in Operating Room." *Journal of the American Medical Association* 62 (June 1914): 1829.

Kanner, Leo. "Art, Music, Recreation Park Features of Unusual Hospital for Insane." *Hospital Management* 22 (September 1926): 46-47, 59.

Katzoff, S. L. "Music an Aid to Health." *National Eclectic Medical Association Quarterly* 13 (December 1921): 135-137.

Kempf, Paul. "Happiness and Health Through Music." *The Musician* 28 (November 1923): 10.

Kennedy, F. S. "Music as a Therapeutic Agent." *Medical Record* 66 (1904): 697.

Kindwall, Josef A. "Heal Through Music." Milwaukee Medical Times 17 (1944): 15-23.

Kirwin, Lillian M. "The Three U's in Music Therapy." *Occupational Therapy and Rehabilitation* 21 (December 1942): 353-356.

Knight, Augustus C. "Why Give Up Your Music?" *The Volta Review* 26 (July 1924): 297-299.

Knott, John. "Music as a Therapeutic Agent." *New England Medical Monthly* 25 (1906): 203-206; see also, *New York Medical Journal* 94 (1911): 678, 727; *Music and Health* 1 (1914): 12-14; and *St. Paul Medical Journal* 8 (1906): 69-76.

Kraft, Ivor. "Music for the Feeble-Minded in Nineteenth-Century America." *Journal of Research in Music Education* 11 (Fall 1963): 119-122.

La Master, Robert J. "Music Therapy as a Tool for Treatment of Mental Patients in the Hospital." *Hospital Management* 62 (December 1946): 110-114.

_____. "Music Therapy as a Tool for Treatment of Mental Patients in the Hospital." *Hospital Management* 63 (January 1947): 111-114.

Larson, B. H. "Music in Medicine." *Journal of the Michigan State Medical Society* 27 (May 1928): 252-256.

Lawrence, Robert M. "The Healing Influence of Music." In *Primitive Psychotherapy and Quackery*. Boston: Houghton Mifflin Co., 1910.

Lederman, Richard. "An Overview of Performing Arts Medicine." *American Music Teacher* 40 (February-March 1991, 12-15, 70-71.

Le Massena, C. E. "Latent Therapeutic Values in Music." *The Musician* 45 (October 1940): 72.

_____. "Music in Therapy." *The Army and Navy Musician* 19 (April-May 1945): 46.

Leslie, R. M., and C. Horsford. "Singing in Its Relation to Pulmonary Consumption." *British Journal of Tuberculosis* 2 (1908): 62.

Lewin, Lucie M. "The Speech Habit." *The Volta Review* 29 (May 1927): 242-244.

Licht, Sidney. "The Place of Music in Hospitals." *MTNA Proceedings* (1948): 255-258.

Light, G. A. "The Use of the Magnetic Recorder." *Anesthesia and Analgesia* 28 (November-December 1949): 330-338.

Lucas, J. "An Account of the Singular Effects of Music on a Patient." *London Medical Journal* 11 (1790): 125-130.

Macomber, Esther. "The Value of Music as Occupational Therapy." *Archives of Occupational Therapy* 3 (April 1924): 125-128.

Maier, Guy. "Music Therapy." *Etude* 62 (November 1944): 624.

Malkiel, Henrietta. "Music, the Medicine." *Musical Digest* 4 (May 1923): 5.

Marke, David Taylor. "Music as Therapeutic Agent Is Advanced by Experiments." *Southern Hospitals* 13 (October 1945): 46.

Marriner, Guy V. R. "Music in Reconditioning in Army Service Forces Hospitals." *Music Library Association Notes* (June 1945): 161-163.

Mason, Guy V. R. "Music in Reconditioning in Army Service Forces Hospitals." *Music Library Association Notes* (June 1945): 161-163.

24

Mathews, Ruth Vendley. "Music for Health: A New Use for the Accordion." *Etude* 55 (March 1937): 199, 203.

Matras, Maud. "Music as Medicine." *Monthly Musical Record* 35 (1905): 168-169.

Mays, Thomas J. "Medicine and Music." *New York Medical Journal* 105 (5 May 1917): 832.

_____. "A Study of Drug Action: Music." *New York Medical Journal* 104 (19 August 1916): 349-351.

_____. "Therapeutic Value of Music." *New York Medical Journal* (August 1918).

McGlinn, John A. "Music in the Operating Room." *American Journal of Obstetrics and Gynecology* 20 (November 1930): 678-683.

McKay, L. A. "Music as a Group Therapeutic Agent in the Treatment of Convalescents." *American Journal of Psychiatry* 100 (May 1944).

"Medical and Surgical Convalescence in Relation to Art and Music." *Clinical Medicine and Surgery* 41 (November 1934): 518-520.

"The Medical Effects of Music." *Literary Digest* 88 (16 January 1926): 25.

"Medical Powers of Music." *The Boston Musical Gazette* 1 (17 October 1838): 99.

"Medical Powers of Music." *The Boston Musical Gazette* 1 (31 October 1838): 106.

"Medical Powers of Music." *The Boston Musical Gazette* 1 (December 1838): 132.

"Medical Powers of Music." *The Musical Magazine* 2 (26 December 1840): 423.

"Medical Powers of Music." *The Musical Magazine* 3 (24 January 1841): 31-32.

"Medical Powers of Music." *The Musical Magazine* 3 (6 February 1841): 45-47.

"Medical Powers of Music." *The Musical Magazine* 3 (6 March 1841): 76-77.

Meese, A. H. "Music, Physical Exercise and Recreation in Mental Diseases." *Occupational Therapy and Rehabilitation* 9 (February 1930): 27-32.

Merz, Charles H. "Music in Medicine." *Cincinnati Lancet-Clinic* 29 (1892): 845-848.

Meyer, E. "Therapeutic Influence of Musical Rhythm on the Parkinsonian Motor Sequelae of Epidemic Encephalitis." *Journal of the American Medical Association* 80 (May 1923): 1493.

Middleton, W. C. "The Effect of Music on Feelings and Restfulness." *Journal of Psychology* (January 1944): 299-328.

Miles, J. R., and C. R. Tilley. "Some Physiological Reactions to Music." *Guy's Hospital Gazette* 49 (August 1935): 319-322.

Mitchell, S. D., and A. Zanker. "Music Styles and Mental Disorders." *Occupational Therapy and Rehabilitation* 28 (October 1949): 411-422.

_____. "The Use of Music in Group Therapy." *Journal of Mental Science* 94 (October 1948): 737-748.

Monro, Sarah A. Jordan. "The Piano as an Aid to Speech." *American Annals of the Deaf* 46 (March 1901): 166-169.

_____. "The Priceless Value of Rhythm to Deaf Children." *The Volta Review* 17 (November 1915): 437-439.

_____. "A Résumé of the Rhythmic Work in the Horace Mann School, Boston." *The Volta Review* 17 ((April 1915): 132-138.

26

_____. "A Plea for the Use of the Piano in Speech and Voice Work." *The Volta Review* 20 (February 1918): 93.

Montani, Angelo. "Psychoanalysis of Music." *Psychoanalytic Review* 32 (April 1945): 225-227.

"More About 'Tom'." *Dwight's Journal of Music* 22 (6 December 1862): 283.

Morton, J. P. "Some Physiological Effects of Jazz and Classical Music." *Bulletin of the University of Pittsburgh* 32 ((1935): 362.

Mott, Frederick. "The Influence of Song on Mind and Body." *Journal of Mental Science* 67 (April 1921): 162-172.

Mueller, Vernette A., and Joseph Mersand. "Music in Educational Reconditioning." *Educational Music Magazine* 25 (November-December 1945): 26-27.

Murtfeld, E. W. "How Music Heals the Sick: Specialists find that Melody Has Weird Effects on Physical Health." *Popular Science* 131 (October 1937): 32-33.

"Music a Means of Preserving Health." *Dwight's Journal of Music* 19 (14 September 1861): 191.

"Music Aids the Anesthetist." *Scientific American* 149 (August 1933): 84.

"Music Among the Blind." *Dwight's Journal of Music* 7 (7 July 1855): 111

"Music Among the Blind." *Dwight's Journal of Music* 9 (6 September 1856): 125.

"Music Among the Blind." *Dwight's Journal of Music* 12 (29 May 1858): 68.

"Music Among the Blind." *Dwight's Journal of Music* 26 (29 September 1866): 319.

"Music Among the Blind." *Dwight's Journal of Music* 29 (24 April 1869): 24.

"Music and Health." *Etude* 50 (November 1932): 780.

"Music and Health: The Curative Powers of Music." *Musical News* 70 (29 May 1926): 457-458.

"Music and Madness." *Etude* 47 (March 1929): 173-174.

"Music and Medicine." *Etude* 55 (August 1937): 492.

"Music and the Blind." *Dwight's Journal of Music* 35 (25 December 1875): 148.

"Music as a Cure All." *Musical Visitor* (June 1888): 317.

"Music as a Cure for Many Ailments." *Current Opinion* 71 (October 1921): 473-474.

"Music as a Medicine." *Chamber's Journal;* 5 (March 1894): 145-146.

"Music as Medicine." *British Medical Journal* (1912): 1380.

"Music as Medicine." *British Musician* 13 (July 1936): 152-154.

"Music as Mind Medicine." *Virginia Medical Monthly* 4 (1877-1878): 920-923.

"Music at the Perkins Institution and Massachusetts Asylum for the Blind." *Dwight's Journal of Music* 36 (9 December 1876): 348-349.

"The Music Cure Among the Indians." *Literary Digest* 77 (June 1923): 30.

"The Music Cure for the Wounded." *Literary Digest* 62 (July 1919): 23-24.

"Music for Health in State Institutions." *Music and Health* 1 (1914): 3-8.

"Music for Shattered Minds." *Literary Digest* 52 (June 1916): 47.

"Music for the Blind." *Dwight's Journal of Music* 3 (9 July 1853): 110.

"Music in Psychoanalysis." *Literary Digest* 114 (1 October 1932): 25.

"Music in Social Education and Mental Treatment." *Occupational Therapy and Rehabilitation* 6 (December 1947): 496.

"Music in the Hospitals." *Literary Digest* 76 (24 February 1923): 68-70.

"Music in Therapy." *National Music Council Bulletin* 6 (September 1945): 20.

"Music May Be Valuable in Mental Treatment." *Hygeia* 13 (July 1935): 669.

"Music Physically Considered." *Columbian Magazine* 111 (February 1789): 90-93.

"Music Used in Therapy." *Scientific Digest* 17 (January 1945): 77.

"Music with the Blind." *Dwight's Journal of Music* 37 (22 December 1877): 147-148.

"Music with the Blind." *Dwight's Journal of Music* 38 (21 December 1878): 353-354.

"Musical Education of the Blind." *Dwight's Journal of Music* 32 (4 May 1872): 227-228.

"Musical Education of the Blind." *Dwight's Journal of Music* 32 (24 (August 1872): 295.

"Musical Prescriptions." *Literary Digest* 62 (August 1919): 26.

"Musical Therapy." *Tri Shield of Phi Mu Gamma* 15 (November 1944): 1.

"Musical Therapy—An Opportunity." *The Musician* 24 (August 12919): 9, 37.

"Music's Part in Fighting Fear." *Etude* 55 (May 1937): 291-292.

"Music's Power to Cure." *Music Life* (November 1902): 25-26.

Narat, Joseph. "Music in Medicine." *Medical Review of Reviews* 38 (1932): 263-267.

"National Association for Music Therapy Convention." *Pan Pipes of Sigma Alpha Iota* 44 ((March 1952): 21, 52.

"National Music Council Report on a Survey on the Use of Music in Hospitals." *National Music Council Bulletin* 5 (January 1945): 7-9.

"National Music Council Report on a Survey on the Use of Music in Hospitals. for Mental and Nervous Diseases." *National Music Council Bulletin* 5 (August 1944): 7-13.

New, Mary. "Rhythm-Work in the Alabama School for the Deaf." *The Volta Review* 23 (April 1921): 148-149.

Newington, H. H. "Some Mental Aspects of Music." *Journal of MEntal Science* 43 (1897): 704-723.

Newlandsmith, Ernst. "Musical Pathology." *Musical Standard* 28 (December 1926): 194.

Nieks, Frederick. "Musical Therapeutics." *Monthly Musical Record* 42 (1912): 3-5.

"Notes from a Patient's Diary." *Punch* (8 June 1895): 267.

"Nothing New About Music for the Sick." *American Weekly* (14 January 1945).

O'Connell, Audree S. "Fifty Years of Music Therapy at the University of the Pacific." *Music Therapy Perspectives* 8 (1990): 90-92.

Olker, P. V. "The Influence of Music in Hospitals." *Bulletin of Iowa Institutions* 2 (1900): 70-72.

30

Osborn, Leslie A. "Response to Musical Therapy." *Mental Hygiene News* 12 (1941-1942): 1.

Owst, Wilberfoss G. "Hemmeter as a Musician and Composer." *Medical Live* 34 (April 1927): 223-224.

Palmer, Martin F., and Louis E. Zerbe. "Control of Athetotic Tremors by Sound Stimuli." *The Journal of Speech Disorders* 10 (1945): 303-319.

Paperte, Frances. "Music in Military Medicine." *Mental Hygiene* 30 (January 1946): 56-64.

Pastnor, Paul. "Music as Medicine." *Music* 15 (1899): 361-365.

Patrici, M. L. "Music and the Cerebral Circulation of Mann--First Experiments." *Music* 11 (1897): 232-242.

Patterson, Mrs. Hugh A. "Techniques for Music in Hospitals." *Music Clubs Magazine* 25 (November -December 1945): 6, 14.

Paul, Doris. "Musicians in White.: *Hygeia* 27 (December 1949): 840.

Paul, Rochelle, and Virginia M. Stadt. "Music Therapy for the Mentally Ill: A Historical Sketch and a Brief Review of the Literature on the Physiological Effects and on Analysis of the Elements of Music." *Journal of General Psychology* 59 (1958): 177-183.

Peet, C. "Music as a Narcotic." *Forum* 57 (August 1930): 113-115.

"Perkins Institute for the Blind." *Dwight's Journal of Music* 40 (3 July 1880): 110-111.

Petrey, E. B. "Music as a Medicine in the Home." *Ladies Home Journal* 20 (October 1903): 49.

"Physical Effects of Music." *Literary Digest* 99 (13 October 1928): 82-83.

Pierce, Appleton H. "The Application of Music in a Veterans' Administration Mental Hospital." *Occupational Therapy and Rehabilitation* 13 (1934): 279-288.

_____. "The Therapeutic Value of Music for Psychotic Patients." *United States Veterans Bureau Medical Bulletin* 11 (October 1934): 142-147.

Plass, Julia. "The Influence of Music on the Patient." *Trained Nurse and Hospital Review* 66 (June 1921): 515-516.

Podolsky, Edward. "Change Your Mood with Music." *Journal of Living* (June 1948): 19.

_____. "The Doctor Looks at Music." *Northwest Musical Herald* 7 (November 1931): 9.

_____. "Effects of Music Upon the Body." *Etude* 38 (June 1940): 411.

_____. "How Music Affects the Human Body." *The Musician* 43 (July 1938): 124.

_____. "How Music Exerts Its Favorable Influence on the Body." *Medical Herald* 49 (September 1930): 328-330.

_____. "Influence of Music on the Body." *Medical World* 43 (1925): 99.

_____. "The Influence of Music on the Circulation of the Blood." *The Medical Times* 58 (October 1930): 300-302.

_____. "The Influence of Music on the Human Body: Historical Incidents." *American Medicine* 37 (February 1931): 99-104; see also *New York Times*, 17 May 1931, Sec. 28, p. 5.

_____. "The Influence of Music Upon the Human Body." *Illinois Medical Journal* 42 (November 1922): 410-413.

_____. "The Influence of Musical Stimuli on the Body." *Trained Nurse and Hospital Review* 87 (November 1931): 613.

32

_____. "Music and Health." *Canadian Medical Association Journal* 30 (February 1934): 195-200; see also *New Health* 9 (December 1934): 18; and *Virginia Medical Monthly* 61 (March 1935): 710-713.

_____. "Music and Mental Health." *The Military Surgeon* 110 (June 1952): 420-423; see also *Music Educators Journal* 40 November-December 1953): 66-70.

_____. "Music and Warped Personalities." *The Stigmatine* 2 (October 1948): 2.

_____. "Music as an Anaesthetic." *Etude* 57 (November 1939): 707.

_____. "Music Becomes a Medicine." *Illinois Medical Journal* 73 (March 1938): 255-258.

_____. "Music Can Work Miracles." *Etude* 58 (August 1940): 514, 562.

_____. "Music in Military Strategy." *Etude* 60 (June 1942): 382.

_____. "Music Keeps the Mind Healthy." *Modern Living* (February 1936): 227.

_____. "Music Rhythm Affects Brain Rhythms." *Etude* 64 (November 1946): 604.

_____. "Music While You Work." *Liberty* (February 1943): 71.

_____. "Music's Role in Healing." *Etude* 51 (July 1933): 442.

_____. "Physical Effects of Musical Vibrations." *The Musician* 47 (May-June 1942): 72.

_____. "The Physical Influence of Music." *Etude* 41 (October 1925): 710.

_____. "Some Aspects of Musical Therapy." *Tomorrow* 1 (November 1941): 33-36.

33

_____. "Some Astonishing Effects of Music Upon the Body." *Etude* 38 (June 1920): 411.

_____. "Some Unusual Effects of Music." *The Musician* 44 (September 1939): 155.

_____. "The Use of Music as a Healing Agent Among the Indians." *Etude* 52 (July 1934): 434; see also *New York Times*, 25 December 1934, Sec. 29, p. 1; and *Cleveland Plain Dealer*, 25 December 1934, p. 8.

Pollack, R. "Medical Men Who Have Loved Music." *Hygeia* 13 (1935): 520-523.

Porter, Sarah Harvey. "Musical Vibrations for the Deaf." *American Annals of the Deaf* 57 (March 1912): 137-158.

Powall, Dorothy Ashby. "To Soothe the Savage Breast." *Ladies Home Journal;* 62 (May 1945): 171-172.

Pratt, Theresa E. "Patients' Libraries and Musical Activities in a Mental Hospital." *Occupational Therapy and Rehabilitation* 19 (December 1940): 379-386.

Rambossam, M. J. "The Influence of Music on the Physical and Moral Nature." *The Lancet* 2 (September 1877): 339.

"Rational Recreation." *Dwight's Journal of Music* 26 (29 September 1866): 316-317.

Reese, Hans H. "The Relation of Music to Diseases of the Brain." *Occupational Therapy and Rehabilitation* 27 (1948): 12-18.

"Remarkable Cure of a Fever by Music: An Attested Fact." *New York Weekly Magazine* 11 (10 August 1796): 44.

"Rhythm." *The Volta Review* 27 (January 1925): 47-49.

Richter, W. G. "The Beneficial Effects of Music for the Mentally Ill." *United States Veterans Bureau Medical Bulletin* 21 (1934): 148-152.

34

Ries, Estelle H. "Using Hidden Senses." *Hygeia* 22 (December 1949): 824-825, 863.

Rigg, M. G. "What Features of a Musical Phrase Have Emotional Suggestiveness?" *Bulletin of the Oklahoma A and M College* (September 1939).

Robertson, Enid. "The Emotional Element in Listening to Music." *Australian Journal of Psychology and Philosophy* 12 (September 1934): 199.

Robinson, Gertrude. "Musical Therapeutics." *Medical Review of Reviews* 24 (1918): 92-94.

Roehman, Franz L., and Suzanne Pierson. "Music and Medicine: A Marginal Interdisciplinary History." *Bulletin of the Council of Research in Music Education* 88 (Summer 1986): 58, 89-90.

Rogers, James F. "The Health of Musicians." *Musical Quarterly* 12 (October 1926).

_____. "Music as Medicine." *Musical Quarterly* 4 (July 1918): 365-375.

Rollin, H. R. "The History of Music Therapy." *History of Medicine* 5 (1973): 15-18.

Rowe, Dorothy B. "Music Makes a Better Nurse." *The Trained Nurse and Hospital Review* 109 (1942): 410-412.

_____. "Musical Therapy: The Application of an Old Art to Modern Medicine." *The Trained Nurse and Hospital Review* (October 1943): 265-268.

Ruegnitz, Marjorie J. "Applied Music on Disturbed Wards." *Occupational Therapy and Rehabilitation* 25 (October 1946): 203-206.

Ryan, Walter B. "Physician Tells How Music Helps the Insane." *Musical America* 30 (May 1919): 42.

Saleeby, Caleb Williams. "Music as Medicine." *Music Journal* 1 (January 1930): 87-88.

_____. "On Music as Medicine." *Music Supervisors Journal* 16 (October 1929): 27-31, 55.

Samuels, Saul S. "Medicine and Music." *Musical Monitor* 14 (February 1924): 13, 25.

Savill, Agnes. "Music and Medicine." *Music and Letters* 4 (July 1923): 282-289.

Schlauffler, Robert Haven. "Music, M.D." *Good Housekeeping* 62 (March 1916): 271-275.

_____. "Musical Pharmacy." *Outlook* 99 (October 1911): 331-335.

Schoen, Max. "Doctoring with Music." *Etude* 60 (March 1942): 166, 200.

Schreiber, Lucille. "Music Hath Charms." *Occupational Therapy and Rehabilitation* 22 (April 1943): 77-80.

Schwartz, A. "Music Therapy." *Quarterly of the Chicago Medical School* 3 (1942-1943): 15.

Scott, George Dow. "The Psychic Value of Music in Infant and Child Nutrition." *Medical Journal and Record* 133 (February 1931`): 161-165, 216-219, 266-269, and 329-330.

Scott, Martha, and Anna L. Week. "Music Found to Have Curative Values for Delinquents and Feebleminded." *Musical America* 49 (25 October 1929): 25-26.

Sear, H. G. "Cure by Music." *West London Medical Journal* 51 (1946): 9-15.

_____. "Music and Medicine." *Music and Letters* 20 (January 1939): 45-54.

Searle, W. Frederic. "Musical Experiment with Patients and Employees at Worcester State Hospital." *Occupational Therapy and Rehabilitation* 12 (1933): 341-356.

Seymour, Harriet Ayer. "Musical Therapy." *Pan Pipes of Sigma Alpha Iota* 36 (May 1944): 171-172.

Shaw, David, and Denis Hill. "A Case of Musicogenic Epilepsy." *Journal of Neurology and Psychopathology* 10 (August 1947): 107-117.

Shehan, Vivian M. "Rehabilitation of Aphasiacs in an Army Hospital." *Journal of Speech Disorders* 11 (June 1946): 149.

Shepherd, Henry Elliott. "The Musical Contributions of a Physiologist." *Medical Life* 34 (April 1927): 219-222.

Shirley, Frances E. "Musical and Dramatic Education of Crippled Children." *The Crippled Child* (August 1955): 48.

Shoemaker, J. V. "The Therapeutic Benefit of Music." *Medical Bulletin* 23 (1901): 290-294.

"Sightless Scholars." *Dwight's Journal of Music* 39 (5 July 1879): 110-111.

Simon Werner. "The Value of Music in the Resocialization and Rehabilitation of the Mentally Ill." *The Military Surgeon* 96 (December 1945): 498-500.

Smith, E. A. "The Influence of Music upon Life and Health." *Music* 8 (1895): 361-365.

Smith, E. S. "Music: Old and New and Its Effects." *The Musician* 45 (March 1940): 46.

"A Society for Hospital Music." *Literary Digest* 89 (May 1926): 24.

Sohmer, Abram. "Music and the Physician." *Phi Delta Epsilon News* 28 (1937): 3-7.

Solomon, Alan L. "Music in Special Education Before 1930: Hearing and Speech Development." *Journal of Research in Music Education* 28 (Winter 1980): 236-242.

Solomon, Alan L., and George N. Heller. "Historical Research in Music Therapy: An Important Avenue for Studying the Profession." *Journal of Music Therapy* 19 (Fall 1982): 161-178.

"Soothing Influence of Music in the Nerves." *The Musician* 22 (August 1917): 577.

Steinberg, Miguel. "Medicine and Music." *Journal of Outdoor Life* (December 1942); see also *Musical Courier* 93 (2 September 1926): 7, 10.

Stevenson, Elwood A. "Musical Rhythm." *American Annals of the Deaf* 64 (May 1919): 196-204.

Stewart, Ollie. "Music That Cures." *Scribner's Commentator* 10 (June 1941): 83-87.

Stokes, W. A. "Music and the Art of Healing." *British Musician* 5 (December 1929): 333-334.

Stratton, Henry W. "The Key-Note in Musical Therapeutics." *Arena* 25 (March 1901): 287-299.

_____. "Music Cure." *Current Literature* 28 (May 1900): 178-180.

Strayer, Edward Ray. "Musical Instruments as an Aid in the Treatment of Muscle Defects and Perversions." *Angle Orthodontist* 9 (April 1939): 18-27.

Sumwalt, R. L. "Music as a Therapeutic Measure." *Musical Courier* 86 (1 February 1923): 7.

Sunderman, Lloyd F. "Study of Some Physiological Differences Between Musicians and Non-Musicians: I. Blood Pressure." *The Journal of Social Psychology* 23 (1946): 205-215.

Sunderman, F. W. "Theodor Billroth as Musician." *Bulletin of the Medical Library Association* 25 (1937): 209-220.

"Surgery to Music." *Literary Digest* 51 (18 December 1915): 1424.

Taylor, Dale B. "Music in General Hospital Treatment from 1900 to 1950." *Journal of Music Therapy* 18 (Summer 1981): 62-73.

Taylor, Selwyn. "A Case of Musicogenic Epilepsy." *Journal of the Royal Navy Medical Service* 28 (October 1942): 394-395.

Terven, Ada. "Musical Therapeutics." *Occupational Therapy and Rehabilitation* 20 (February 1941): 31-34.

"Therapeutic Value of Music." *New York Times*, 25 September 1932, Sec. 6, p. 4.

"The Therapeutic Value of Music for Psychotic Patients." *U. S. Veterans Bureau Medical Bulletin* 11 (October 1934): 142-147.

"The Therapeutic Value of Music in Hospitals: Doubts and Insinuations." *Hospital Topics and Buyers* 4 (January 1927): 30.

Thomas, C. Edgar. "Music as a Cure for Disease." *Musical Courier* 72 (1916): 29-30.

Thomason, Pattie. "Voice Training for Deaf Children." *The Volta Review* 20 (June 1918): 311-314.

Thompson, B. A. "Say It with Music." *Occupational Therapy and Rehabilitation* 11 (October 1932): 383.

Tilly, Margaret. "The Psychoanalytical Approach to the Masculine and Feminine Principles in Music." *The American Journal of Psychiatry* 103 (January 1947): 477-483.

Tindall, G. M. "Rhythm for the Restless." *Personnel Journal* 16 (October 1937): 120.

Treves, Norman E. "A Study of the Effects of Music on Cancer Patients." *Hospital Social Services* 16 (August 1927): 123-131.

Turner, Walter James. "Music and Health." *New Statesman* 33 (18 May 1929): 181-182.

Turner, William W., and David E. Bartlett. "Music Among the Deaf and Dumb." *American Annals of the Deaf and Dumb* 2 (October 1848): 1-6.

Underwood, Roy. "The Human Response to Music." *MTNA Proceedings* (1946): 356-359.

_____. "Music in Therapy." *Education* 67 (November 1946): 157-161.

"Value of Music Therapy Discussed." *New York Times*, 21 October 1945, Sec. 2, p. 4.

Van Adestine, Gertrude. "A Cross-Section of a Day's Work in the Detroit Day School." *The Volta Review* 29 (March 1927): 138-139.

Van de Wall, Willem. "Enrichment of Adult Life Thru Music." *Proceedings of the National Education Association* (1933): 290-293.

_____. "Functional Use of Music in Industry and Therapy." *MTNA Proceedings* (1944): 147-153.

_____. "How Music Is Saving Thousands from Permanent Mental Breakdown." *Etude* 43 (September 1925): 613-614.

_____. "Music an Emotional Asset." *The Musician* 40 (February 1935): 4, 12.

_____. "Music and Physical Well Being." *The Musician* 43 (October 1938): 169, 177.

_____. "Music as a Means of Mental Discipline." *Archives of Occupational Therapy* 2 (February 1923): 126.

40

_____. "Music: Boon or Bane?" *Modern Hospital* 64 (June 1945): 79-80.

_____. "Music for Sub-Normal Children of the Public Schools." *Etude* 47 (January 1929): 28.

_____. "Music in General Hospitals." *The Modern Hospital* 21 (December 1923): 564-568.

_____. "Music in Hospitals." In *Music and Medicine*, ed. Dorothy M. Schullian and Max Schoen, 293-321. New York: Henry Schuman, 1948.

_____. "Music in the Classroom of the Problem Child." *Etude* 48 (May 1930): 326, 372.

_____. "Music in the Treatment of Retarded Children." *Music Supervisors Journal* 14 (May 1928): 49.

_____. "Music Therapeutics in a Mental Hospital." *Long Island Medical Journal* 17 (May 1928): 221-222.

_____. "Music's Mission in Correctional Personality Reconstruction." *Annual Report of the Prison Association of New York* (1923).

_____. "The Musician's Contribution to Modern Medical Treatment." *Occupational Therapy and Rehabilitation* 5 (February 1926): 79.

_____. "Physio-Motor Reactions to Music." *The Musician* 43 (September 1938): 156.

_____. "Program on Institutions for Mentally Deficient." *Proceedings of the American Association for the Study of the Feeble-Minded* 56 (1932): 70-98.

_____. "The Psychotherapeutic Value of Music." *The Playground* 19 (July 1925): 200-202, 220-223.

_____. "A Systematic Music Program for Mental Hospitals." *American Journal of Psychiatry* 6 (October 1926): 279-291.

_____. "Use of Music in Social Education." *The Musician* 43 (September 1938): 140-141.

Van de Wall, Willem, and Earl D. Bond. "The Use of Music in a Case of Psychoneurosis." *American Journal of Psychiatry* 91 (September 1934): 287-302.

Vescelius, Eva A. "Music and Health." *Musical Quarterly* 4 (July 1918): 376-401.

_____. "Music for Health in State Institutions." *Music and Health* 1 (June 1913): 4-8.

_____. "Music for the Blind." *Music and Health* 1 (June 1913): 15-17.

_____. "Music in Its Relation to Life." *Music and Health* 1 (1914): 5-10.

Vescelius, Louise. "Music Attuned to the Patient's Pulse Beat a Life Renewer." *Musical America* (10 May 1919): 3-4.

Vincent, Esther H. "The Doctors Look at Music." *Quarterly Bulletin of the Northwestern University Medical School* 20 (Summer 1946): 240-246.

Vincent, Swale, and J. H. Thompson. "Effects of Music Upon the Human Blood Pressure." *Lancet* 1 (March 1929): 534-537.

Wade, Beatrice D. "The Future of Music as a Therapeutic Medium." *Trained Nurse and Hospital Review* 124 (February 1950): 60-61, 90.

Wainwright, J. W. "Music as a Remedial Agent." *Dietetics and Hygiene Gazette* 22 (1906): 12-14.

Walden, Sylvia. "Music for the Mentally Disturbed." *Etude* 63 (May 1945): 263, 292.

Wallian, S. S. "Music and Medicine." *Musical Courier* (22 January 1902): 34.

Ward, Milton H. "Note on Psychomusic and Musical Group Psycho-Therapy." *Sociometry* 8 (August 1945): 238-241.

Warlow, Mary. "Striking Modern Ideas on Music as a Curative Force." *Etude* 30 (May 1913): 326.

Warthin, Aldred Scott. "Some Physiologic Effects of Music in Hypnotized Subjects." *Medical News* 65 (28 July 1894): 89-92.

Waugh, Mildred Ockert. "Music in the Post-War Therapy." *Medical Women's Journal* 53 (April 1946): 49, 70.

Weare, M. C. "Health to the Pupil Through Music." *The Musician* 25 (January 1920): 9, 36.

Wecker, Karl. "Music for Totally Deaf Children." *Music Educators Journal* 25 (May 1939): 45-46.

Week, Anna L. "Music as a Healing Art." *Musical Leader* 57 (1929): 13.

Weinfield, E. "Medical Men Who Have Attempted Fame in Other Fields of Endeavor. I. Medical Men as Musicians." *Annals of Internal Medicine* 3 (1930): 1046-1054.

Wells, Maie Lounsbury. "Breaking Mental Barriers." *Welfare Magazine* 19 (1928): 480-488.

White, Mary Louisa. "The Power of Tone, Its Emotional and Colour Rousing Impressiveness." *Musical Standard* 32 (1909): 148-149.

Whiteford, J. W. "Music and Medicine." *University of Manitoba Medical Journal* 12 (1940-41): 50.

Whitely, Paul L. "The Influence of Music on Memory." *Journal of General Psychology* 10 (January 1934): 137-151.

Whitford, Homer. "Music Therapy New Field of Opportunity to the Organist." *Diapason* 33 (7 October 1942): 7.

Whiting, H. S. "Effect of Music on Hospital Accident Rate." *American Journal of Mental Deficiency* 51 (January 1947): 397-400.

Whittaker, J. T. "Music as a Medicine." *Clinic* 6 (1874): 289-294.

Wiant, W. R. "Medicine in Music." *West Virginia Medical Journal* 37 (November 1941): 508-509.

Wiedman, F. E. "Music as a Therapeutic Agent." *Transactions of the Indiana Medical Society* 54 (1903): 190-193.

Williams, Richard. "Music for What Ails You." *House Beautiful* 85 (October 1943): 37, 113-114.

Wimmer, Sebastian. J. "The Influence of Music and Its Therapeutic Value." *New York Medical Journal* 1 (1889).

Winship, A. E. "Music for Mentally Crippled Children." *Music Supervisors Journal* 14 (May 1928): 47, 85.

Witherspoon, Herbert. "Music in Therapeutics." *Musical Digest* 14 (February 1929): 31, 52, 54.

Wittenberg, R. "Psychiatric Concepts in Group Work Applied Through Media of Drama and Music." *American Journal of Orthopsychiatry* 14 (January 1944): 76-83.

Yearsley, Macleod. "Music as a Treatment in Elizabethan Medicine." *Lancet* 1 (February 1935): 415-416.

Zbinden, T. "The Value of Music to the Physician." *MTNA Proceedings* (1915), 264-271.

III. DISSERTATIONS

Boxberger, Ruth. "A Historical Study of the National Association for Music Therapy." Ph.D. diss., The University of Kansas, 1963.

Davis, William B. "An Analysis of Selected Nineteenth-Century Music Therapy Literature." Ph.D. diss., The University of Kansas, 1984.

Diserens, Chares M. "The Influence of Music on Behavior." Ph.D. ddiss., University of Cincinnati, 1922.

Johnson, Robert E. "E. Thayer Gaston: Contributions to Music Therapy and Music Education." Ph.D. diss., The University of Michigan, 1973.

Kersten, Fred G. "An Analysis of Music Education Methods and Materials for the Visually Impaired Synthesized from Documents Written Between 1891 and 1978." D.Ed. diss., The Pennsylvania State University, 1979.

Kraft, Ivor. "Education for Idiots: Caring for the Mentally Retarded in Nineteenth-Century America." Ph.D. diss., Johns Hopkins University, 1962.

Solomon, Alan L. "A Historical Study of the National Association for Music Therapy, 1960-1980." Ph.D. diss., The University of Kansas, 1984.

Washco, Alec. "The Effects of Music Upon Pulse Rate, Blood Pressure, and Mental Imagery." Ed.D. diss., Temple University, 1933.

IV. THESES

Alexander, Jennie L. "The Use of the Piano with the Deaf." Master's thesis, Gallaudet College, 1932.

AlLee, Bonnie L. "A Historical Study of Music Therapy." Master's thesis, University of Arizona, 1954.

Bailey, Phyllis. "Pitch Discrimination in Frequency Areas with Hearing Losses." Master's thesis, University of Minnesota, 1942.

Bell, Alice H. "Some Aspects of the Therapeutic Use of Music with Patients in the Psychopathic Hospital." Master's thesis, The University of Iowa, 1938.

Breitenbach, Ruth A. "A Study of Music in the Public Schools for Physically Handicapped Children." Master's thesis, New York University, 1932.

Downing, Marion L. "A Study of Rhythmic Responses in Totally Deaf Children." Master's thesis, The University of Kansas, 1948.

Eberle, Vivian G. "A Study of the Use of Music for the Socially Deficient and Mentally Gifted in Several Institutions in Ohio." Master's thesis, The Ohio State University, 1944.

Englehardt, Helen L. "Music in Mental Institutions." Master's thesis, The University of Kansas, 1941.

Ferguson, Margaret C. "The History of Music Therapy." Master's thesis, Wayne State University, 1952.

Griffin, Martha R. "Music as a Therapeutic." Master's thesis, Arthur Jordan Conservatory of Music, 1945.

46

Guelig, Evangeline. "The Effects of Music on the Socially Maladjusted." Master's thesis, Northwestern University, 1943.

Harbert, Wilhelmina K. "Some Principles, Practices, and Techniques in Music Therapy." Master's thesis, College of the Pacific, 1947.

Harms, David. "Music in California State Institutions." Master's thesis, College of the Pacific, 1939.

Hess, Robert. "The Therapeutic Value of Music." Master's thesis, Illinois Wesleyan University, 1938.

Horner, Barbara Phyllis. "Mood Music as a Therapeutic Aid." Master's thesis, Northwestern University, 1947.

Judge, Betty Ann. "Continuation of Music as a Therapy." Bachelor's thesis, New England Conservatory of Music, 1944.

Kaplan, Pauline. "Types of Listeners and Listening and Their Application to Music Therapy." Master's thesis, Michigan State College, 1948.

Kilpatrick, Marion W. "An Investigation of the Relationship Between Acuity of Hearing and Handedness in High School." Master's thesis, Syracuse University, 1943.

King, Gwendolyn N. "Musical Experiences to Aid Mexican Bilingual Children in Correcting Speech Defects." Master's thesis, University of Arizona, 1946.

Lambach, Hugo C. "Music as an Adjunct to Medical Therapeutics and Prognosis." Master's thesis, Northwestern University, 1947.

Laughlin, Lynn Ann. "The Development of the Music Therapy Program at The University of Kansas from Its Inception Through 1971." Master's thesis, The University of Kansas, 1974.

Lopatin, Arnold. "A Report of a Music Therapy Program Organized at New Jersey State Hospital." Master's thesis, Michigan State College, 1947.

Lord, Dorothy. "Teaching Music to the Deaf in the Elementary School." Master's thesis, The Ohio State University, 1935.

McCuskey, Alice E. "Teaching Piano to the Visually Handicapped." Master's thesis, The Ohio State University, 1944.

Peery, John C. "Music for Retarded Boys." Master's thesis, University of Idaho, 1942.

Perry, Doradeen. "A Study of the Effects of Music in the Learning of Braille by Seeing Subjects." Master's thesis, The University of Kansas, 1945.

Rogers, Sara E. "A Study of and Curriculum for Music in Feeble-Minded Institutions." Master's thesis, George Peabody College for Teachers, 1936.

Roth, Gertrude. "An Experimental Study of the Development and Effect of a Program of Music Study on Mentally Retarded Children in the Public Schools." Master's thesis, The University of Iowa, 1942.

Roucaglione, V. "Music in Therapy." Master's thesis, West Virginia University, 1947.

Rowan, James M. "A History of Music Therapy in Topeka, Kansas from 1881 Through 1956." Master's thesis, The University of Kansas, 1984.

Sanderson, Alice. "The Status of Music Instruction in Schools for the Blind in the United States." Master's thesis, Northwestern University, 1933.

Schrader, Bonita M. "An Investigation Concerning the Effects of Music on Health." Master's thesis, University of Denver, 1929.

Sherrad, Wayne. "Therapeutics Through Music." Master's thesis, Teachers College, Columbia University, 1939.

Sisson, Clarawanda. "Music as a Therapeutic Agent." Master's thesis, The University of Michigan, 1940.

48

Sporny, Vetold W. "Value of Music in Correctional Institutions." Master's thesis, Duquesne University, 1941.

Stolz, Elizabeth. "Reactions of a Group of Elementary Children in a Residence School for the Blind to a Modern Education Program." Master's thesis, The Ohio State University, 1939.

Tatgenhorst, Ted C. "Functional Music in the School Program." Master's thesis, Stanford University, 1946.

Taylor, Lura. "Music Appreciation Through Bone-Conduction." Master's thesis, New England Conservatory of Music, 1936.

Tull, Maxine. "What Music Means to the Deaf Child." Master's thesis, Gallaudet College, 1926.

Turansky, Robert. "Music as Therapy in Mental Illness." Master's thesis, Duquesne University, 1948.

Weber, Clayton. "A Study of Auditory Acuity of School Children." Master's thesis, Syracuse University, 1938.

Zehetner, Arthur W. "The Healing Power of Music." Master's thesis, Western Reserve University, 1934.